DIGITAL MINIMALISM

AF570057

DR DHEERAJ MEHROTRA

Copyright © Dr Dheeraj Mehrotra
All Rights Reserved.

This book has been published with all efforts taken to make the material error-free after the consent of the author. However, the author and the publisher do not assume and hereby disclaim any liability to any party for any loss, damage, or disruption caused by errors or omissions, whether such errors or omissions result from negligence, accident, or any other cause.

While every effort has been made to avoid any mistake or omission, this publication is being sold on the condition and understanding that neither the author nor the publishers or printers would be liable in any manner to any person by reason of any mistake or omission in this publication or for any action taken or omitted to be taken or advice rendered or accepted on the basis of this work. For any defect in printing or binding the publishers will be liable only to replace the defective copy by another copy of this work then available.

Contents

Preface

Digital Minimalism activates an appreciation of how much of a digital footprint one has to have as a gentleman's promise.

It salutes the amount necessary as how much is too much as intelligence. Let us clean out our electronic cobwebs and digital dust bunnies so we can enjoy our digital minimalism. The requisite is the need of the hour.

I am sure the readers would like it informative and meaningful.

Happy Reading.

Cheers

www.authordheerajmehrotra.com

ONE

Digital Minimalism- What & Why?

Hi Guys,

Digital Minimalism is like how much is too much? As a priority, being a digital minimalist will reduce your time spent on digital devices and improve your quality of life by providing more meaning and value to the things around you. It will also improve your concentration at work and home, particularly prioritising learning. You'll be able to filter items of little to no importance to you. Out of the preface, Digital Minimalism, the approach activates an appreciation of how much of a digital footprint one must have as a gentleman's promise. We tend to reflect on how we start our day by checking our devices, the alarm, the reminders and the updates. How far and fair is the dependence? This is indeed a way to bring undiluted excuses to our way of life and the reaction to each comment or even the likes.

Cal Newport's definition of digital minimalism: *"Digital minimalism is a philosophy that helps you question what digital communication tools (and behaviours surrounding these tools) add the most value to your life. It is motivated by the belief that intentionally and aggressively clearing away low-value digital noise and optimising your use of the matter tools can significantly improve your life." Taking a note from his comments* *on the ease of doing things and reacting to the reaction of others, there is an emergent nurturing of others to showcase and reflect on others.*

It salutes the amount necessary as how much is too much as intelligence. Let us clean out our electronic cobwebs and digital dust bunnies so we can enjoy our digital minimalism. The requisite is the need of the hour. A check with reference dilutes to define the term Digital Minimalism just as not a rejection or a setback of technology and all of its pros in particular; it's about being intentional and mindful about and, as a matter of fact, with our use of technology so that it helps us instead confuses and puzzles us towards further planned assignments/ work at our workplace rather.

It talks fun and wit at times that being a digital minimalist will reduce time encapsulated on digital platforms and improve your quality of life by providing more meaning and value to the things around you. It will also improve your concentration, and you'll be able to filter items of little to no importance to you in totality. Minimalist technology uses the "less is more" principle for the digital products we need. Minimalism in a digital world can decrease distraction, save time, and increase organisation and productivity. As a part of digital minimalism, if you regularly clear your cookies, the web will be more annoying. You'll see the same messages again that you've already earned, and sites will keep asking you to log back in. Your browser usually has good reasons for storing cookies and other private data. Being a digital minimalist will reduce your time spent on digital devices and improve your quality of life by providing more meaning and value to the things around you. It will also improve your concentration, and you'll be able to filter items of little to no importance. Source: https://www.apartmenttherapy.com/10-ways-to-simplify-your-digit-164026 quotes a fascinating fact about being digital but with minimalism.

Worth quoting the fact:

In a studio apartment, with its tiny closets and even tinier kitchen cabinets, it's essential to be disciplined about clearing clutter. But online? Where does your Gmail inbox have seemingly endless storage space, and can you hide your hoarding "in the cloud"? It's easy to amass an insurmountable pile of digital junk. The salutations tend to reflect and say, with the preface of incidences, with a loaded dependence on technology, like these might indicate that our very use of technology is getting framed as an obstacle towards the planned goals and operations. And if that's the case, it could be valuable to take the idea of Digital Minimalism a little more seriously. Well, as Thomas Edison rightly says, "Five per cent of the people think; ten per cent of the people think they think, and the other eighty-five per cent would rather die than think."

Here are ten small tasks you can start today, tomorrow or on a lazy weekend morning to help you clean up your online and digital life.

1. Get set to a minimum of two Email Accounts while working online and managing your email accounts. This may include, One work and one home email address. That's all you need. If you're still hanging on to your university account or an inbox from an old job, take steps to eliminate them. Move over important contact information and forward any valuable emails to your primary address. When you're sure, you've got all you need, close the accounts for good.

2. Get into a habit of Uninstalling the Unused Software from your computer desktop. Delete your inbox of no use. Clear your JUNK folders on the move.

3. Purge your Mobile Device App Library. This is so much very required for non-used folders and files. While cleaning out software from your laptop, make sure your mobile devices get the same love. Go through your smartphone or tablet to clear out those games, shortcuts, and "productivity boosters" you never use anymore. In addition to all the settings which go by default, The tried-and-true method for deleting apps from your Android phone or tablet is simple: Long-press on the app's icon until the app shortcut's popup shows up. You'll see an "i" button or App Info; tap it. Next, select Uninstall.

We are best guided to do so for the iPhone help or support via: Head to the App Library section by scrolling past the last page on your home screen. Now long-press on a space in the App Library to enter jiggle mode or edit mode. Now, tap on the "X" icon to delete it from your iPhone next to any app. When prompted, choose "Delete" to confirm, and here you go!

4. Reflect as a priority on Deleting Old Documents. Open your computer's documents folder and sort everything by "date modified." If you haven't touched that spreadsheet in over a year, it's time to purge it from your machine. Save the stuff you think you might need onto an external hard drive designated for an unorganised "dump", and permanently delete the rest. On the mobiles, Tap Menu. Tap Settings. Tap Privacy & security. Tap Clear cache and Clear all cookie data.

5. Clear Your Computer Desktop. How many icons are on your desktop right now? If you can't finish counting them on two hands, it's time to sift through them. Move often-used programs to your taskbar or dock, and sort all your documents within a single folder. Soon you'll find a clean desktop that can be as calming as a clean kitchen.

6. Cancel Accounts on Unused Social Sites: The priority counts with reflection. Visit the website's support website and look for information on deleting accounts. You may also want to check the website's privacy policy for specific details about when the company deletes data and how you can request deletion. Contact the website's support and ask to delete the account. Thus, after hearing about "Minimalism", many consider claiming a couple of devices for ease, comfort and structure, a minimalistic home with only bedding and zero waste. This couldn't be further away from reality. Minimalism has barely anything to do with the stuff. Things are only a result of a mentality. Minimalism is about attitude. It's tied in with living with aim. You make room — reality — for the things you love and kill all that diverts us from them. You become deliberate with what you decide to do and claim and how it influences as you would prefer of living, thinking, and point of view on life. As a dependent user of technology, you check Facebook every day. But how often do you travel over to LinkedIn? Keeping profiles on social sites, you never visit can be a security risk, not a big waste of mental space. If it's the site where you need a password reminder each time you visit, do yourself a favour and click the "close account" button.

7. Change Your Notification Settings. This is of much importance. Now that you're only subscribed to sites you visit often, you don't need notifications to alert you of a new photo tag or direct message. Change your alert settings to the bare minimum, and you'll be clearing out your email or text message inbox simultaneously. You might be more productive at work without Facebook popping up on your phone's screen every two seconds.

8. Clean Up Your Browser, When you use a browser like Chrome, it saves some information from websites in its cache and cookies. Clearing them fixes specific problems, like loading or formatting issues on sites. The Browser plug-ins are the doughnut holes of the online world; they're easy and harmless to add on one by one, but you've tacked some serious weight to your toolbar before you know it. Clean up your web browser of choice by deleting all but the necessary plug-ins, toolbars and add-ons. Make your web experience as minimalist as possible.

9. Unsubscribe from Unneeded Email Lists via Subscribing to a store's email list for the free 20 per cent off coupon you get for joining is smart shopping. But staying subscribed to a list when you don't even open the emails before deleting them is stupid. Make this week your purge week, and click "unsubscribe" at the bottom of each email as it comes in.

10. Clean Up Your Contacts as a matter of priority, say that using Siri on the iPhone 4S has brought a big problem: When we say "ring Sarah," Siri has to weed through about 12 people to figure out who we want to call. It's time we rid ourselves of unused contacts from old coworkers, long-lost friends and ex-relationships—anyone you haven't spoken to within over a year is fair game.

In addition, what matters is also working online through a strategy. Unsubscribe, unfollow or delete anything that doesn't "add value." For example, if I follow a YouTuber who regularly pops up on my feed but hasn't clicked on their videos in a couple of months, I might unsubscribe from their channel because their content is not adding value to it live right now.

Now, please know I am not advocating for simply turning off anything that feels uncomfortable. Sometimes we need to lean into complex topics and do the hard work required to learn about the world and how to modify our behaviour. I advocate consuming content healthily for you, which brings me to my next point. Subscribe to things that do "add value." After removing all the clutter from your feed, you can think about subscribing to a couple of things that will add the kind of content that feels good to consume or helps you somehow. The minimalism of digital format signifies the change in habits which ultimately change a life.

Turn off notifications. If you find yourself constantly dismissing emails from a particular brand or feeling irritated by the number of Facebook notifications you receive, take a few minutes and toggle those notifications off within each app or website. I know it can feel a little tedious, but trust me - it's well worth the time investment. I worry about the learning which goes with our reflections, otherwise of working online and depending too much on the devices at large.

Digital minimalism is similar to conventional ideas of minimalism: clearing away clutter so you can focus on what matters most. We usually think of this in the context of physical goods, but it applies to digital stuff. And because we live in a world where we are constantly using apps and websites that are designed to lure us in and suck our attention the same way slot machines do by getting us stuck in a "wanting / liking" dopamine and opioid loop, it's so important to know how to take back control of your online and digital experience. Disappointment. Outrage. Stress. Overpowering wreck. In a nutshell, It's cleaning up your digital life to use just what you need in the most efficient way possible otherwise.

Looking for a document is like searching for that shirt you realise you washed. Is it still in the dryer? Did you pass on it in a heap on the couch to be collapsed? Is it on the pressing board to be pressed? Stand by! Did you even move that heap into the dryer? Or was it essentially lost between your washer and your wardrobe?

While you are not stumbling over your advanced life as you do with clothing, it is often a similar inclination. An immense heap sucks your mental ability, time, and cash. At the point when you genuinely do endeavour to manage it, you end up wildly looking for all that you have stowing away in your PCs, the cloud, SD cards, USBs, and outside hard drives. In last-minute endeavours, you start frantically erasing photographs, recordings, and archives, trusting you are not erasing anything significant, everything so you can track down space to take a couple more pictures or shoot only another moment of the video.

In addition, Digital Declutter is being made possible via cleaning your desktop, clearing your downloads folder, organising documents folders, renaming documents, backing up files to the cloud servers, deleting unused applications, emptying the recycle bins, clearing cookies and cache, deleting any new extensions, cleaning out the bookmarks folders, clear the junk folders of emails, clearing the bin folders, unread emails, unsubscribe from unwanted email lists, subscriptions, sorting the mails into category wise folders, deleting the unwanted text and threads of emails, organising the files into folders, apps into folders, updating the software, backing up the files or photos to the cloud in addition to checking memberships.

You should delete them and other data after your session using a public computer, such as browsing history. We recommend clearing all cookies at least once a month if it's your device. Also, you should do this if you see a drop in browser performance or after visiting a shady website. Once you understand your actual values, you can build your technology use around them. Rather than feeling overwhelmed, you become more intentional, empowered, and productive.

Your distraught cleaning up under pressure or going away from being too digital through connection with technology or the adoption of technology, for sure, doesn't assist you with dealing with your large, muddled heaps of advanced mess. You are losing time to unfortunate work processes and looking for documents. You ask yourself which account you saved that task in. How long have you lost in your life looking for lost documents? You realise they are in there, hanging out on the internet.

Managing passwords is yet another hell of an affair. You realise you saved it someplace. If by some good luck you could recall where it was or, on the other hand, if you labelled it appropriately. Couldn't it be perfect assuming you had a framework to take care of your documents and effectively determine the following opportunity you looked for? You get eternal updates from organisations that your capacity runs short, expanding your interruptions over the day. Do your books send you messages that they are jumbling the family room? Not. Do the dispersed Legos in the lounge area let you know they are awkward? Not by and large, yet we, in all actuality, do know when we step on them, stumbling over the different pieces and hitting our toes.

Digital minimalism is one way we can make sure we are in control of our devices instead of them controlling us. Get a habit of Better focusing. Fewer distractions mean better focus! For me, this is a major stress-reducer. It means I am more productive, which helps boost my confidence and reduce my task list, and I can get "in the flow" while working on things I love, like writing!

Give your mind a rest. And for me, a rested mind means less anxiety and more happiness. Curate a feed that adds real value for you. Your time and energy are precious, and you should protect them by ensuring the things that get your attention to add value for you.

The priority counts on Organising your digital clutter from your travels around the world wide web. To prioritise working for self, one has to Right-size the digital assets with digital storage. Explore the learning toward the skills for healthy digital habits and online reputation management. The successful launch indicates the provision, which activates the prolific nature of learning as a priority.

However much I can give tips and suggestions for how you can rehearse advanced moderation, at last, you want to figure out how to rehearse it that functions for you. Clearing your browser history is NOT the same as clearing your Google Web & App Activity. When you remove your browser history, you're only deleting the locally stored history on your computer. Clearing your browser history doesn't do anything to the data stored on Google's servers.

You know your cutoff points and what you can participate in given your living conditions at a given second. Now and then, you can accomplish more; once in a while, you can do less. That is thoroughly fine and human. One of my number one statements is "figure out how to rest, not to stop", and I imagine that applies here, particularly regarding consuming substances on the web. It's alright to enjoy reprieves however long you want if you don't block out what's happening on the planet.

In addition, clearing the browser history is such a priority too! Your browser tends to hold onto information, which can cause problems with logging in to or loading websites over time. It is always good to clear your cache or browser history and clear cookies regularly. To remove the web cache while keeping the browsing history saved, only the box cached images and files are checked in the Clear browsing data window. Then click the Clear data button. Only the browser cache will be cleared, while the browsing history and cookies will be saved. The data, The information stockpiling organisations, realise you can't see your messiness, so they need to send you messages repeatedly to tidy up your information wreck!

Ponder those heaps of photos filling their capacity units alongside the old tax documents you've checked and that fantastic show you gave working the previous fall. There is probably an old, deserted blog, as well. You're presumably not prepared for crises. In case of a fire, storm, or flood, you require your computerised resources to remain careful. You should take photographs of your assets for the insurance agency and store them in the cloud. Also, when we talk about the sense of working, pondering over what we do by being online? Some of the activities which reduce our creativity are our CLOUD WINDOW SHOPPING and checking the status, pictures which never get to the public eye, the capacities of entertainment and the honour in life about others via their posts and lets us decide about what and how to react and respond by either a phone call or just a like or a comment in totality.

The constant digital interface is so much of importance is a myth. Can't we survive not checking our status on social media? The dependence causes the perplexing nature of being as possible additional gadgets and ropes spread around your home, the vehicle, and work areas. You likely have heaps of old and new devices alongside every one of the ropes, chargers, and different frills that go with them. In addition, you purchased the additional lines because you lost one of them and the other extra strings you bought.

After all, it was abandoned when you disappeared on vacation. The extra charging ropes you've forgotten at home that you wanted for work excursions. To clear things out, it's not a bad idea to do a Remove All on cookies every few months. A comic relief talk about DIGITAL BEGGING has to have the spectrum of asking or sharing the digital passwords and user IDs like that of NETFLIX, Amazon Prime or Hotstar.

Cleaning up your equipment will assist you with seeing what you have for outer capacity choices, with additional strings, chargers, and embellishments going towards your crisis readiness. It can turn into a mind-boggling cerebral pain of headache levels to try and ponder handling the wreck of your advanced life.

The odds are good that you are predominantly lost on the best way to manage everything. Choices escape you; selection weakness has set up house and is picking paint tones. You want to assume control over this wreck deliberately. Outcomes situated housekeeping framework assists you with taking control over your existing domain. It is such a damn story when we tend to realise productivity via the cloud.

When your digital clutter stresses you out, the recommendation of a digital detox is often given, meaning a total break away from your digital life with complete rest. The only problem with the usual detox methods is that when you turn the power back on again to your digital life, all the clutter is still there, most of which caused the stress in the first place. You may have tried several digital detox sessions thinking it would help. Still, it doesn't because you return to the same situation you left: a big black hole of data filled with files and photos of your digital life from the past five, ten, or even twenty years! It's much easier to be passive-aggressive about the mess and just shut your device down.

It is overwhelming to think about how much digital stuff has permeated our lives. I feel that if we had control over all this stuff, a digital detox wouldn't be necessary! Therefore, your files and accounts need to be maintained. What and why? As a priority in life. Technology readiness has caused confusion and change in the lifestyle otherwise. Our lunch timings have changed, late-night working has taken a new clock, skip of breakfast by the Millennials, also known as Generation Y or Gen Y, are the demographic cohort following Generation X and preceding Generation Z, is so damn common now. Josh Millburn & Ryan Nicodemus, two bloggers largely credited with kickstarting the current Minimalist movement, define it like this: Minimalism is a lifestyle that helps people question what things add value to their lives. By clearing the clutter from life's path, we can all make room for the most important aspects of life: health, relationships, passion, growth, and contribution. The key idea is that Minimalism isn't about less; it's about more. Choosing to own fewer things is simply a means of clarifying and focusing on our values so we can fill our lives with more of the things that truly matter to us. Quote/ Unquote!

Additionally, the time has come to take control of your computerised domain! Computerised cleaning up is more than eliminating overabundance and solidifying advanced resources. It's also about right-estimating your applications, resources, capacity, and gadgets. You must use every product's elements to infer the most advantages for your time and cash.

In addition, set up filters in Gmail to automatically sort your email for yourself, archive all the social media notification emails, create a second email account to use when signing up for the freebies and use OneTab to save all 14 tabs you have open at the moment and have your browser run faster, turn off notifications on Facebook posts you no longer follow, keep the Facebook posts you want to refer back to later, in addition, use Google Voice

Typing in Google docs to write posts faster, use cloud storage like that of Google Photos to store the pictures off your phone and clean up the space, use the digital bar in the notes section to organise your thoughts and write down the quick ideas, make sure, you clean up your desktop and places your files and icons in the correct folders in particular.

The challenge to overcoming digital minimalism targets easing the work and the home balance. During the first and the last hour of your day, let the phone be in silent mode, relax, meditate, journal your thoughts, and drink coffee. On another day, just for a change, turn off your phone for the afternoon, try a new workout routine with a friend instead, limit the use of social media only for 30 minutes and try cooking a fresh, healthy meal. Let you be away from the phones on Sundays and instead explore a part of the town you have not before. Go for a nature hike with a friend, or write your goals for the future instead.

The ways to attain digital minimalism are also reflected via staying offline for a day, evaluating your commitments, taking a step towards learning a new skill, unfollowing and unfriending, turn off notifications. Digital minimalism is a way to clearly define what technologies you let into your life and how you use them.

Once you understand your actual values, you can build your technology use around them. Rather than feeling overwhelmed, you become more intentional, empowered, and productive. As a priority, being a minimalist is a time of need for the majority. For sure, by becoming or acting like a minimalist, one essentially reduces the time and the stress associated with doing the job as part and parcel of the job and the environment. Becoming a minimalist dramatically reduces the time and anxiety associated with moving homes. You'll spend much less time packing boxes, hauling items in a moving truck and setting up your new home when you own fewer possessions, making home moves much more accessible.

Quoting, https://nickwignall.com/what-is-digital-minimalism/ I wish to agree that, In particular, there's a version of Minimalism called Digital Minimalism that's quickly rising to prominence as our lives become increasingly tech-centric. Personal technology like smartphones and tablets enables us to spend more and more time online. It is like how much is too much and how much is sufficient to control and review. The idea is towards making work a priority but balancing the use of technology in our lives. It should and must never seize take over our lives.

The activation features mark the understanding in view, with many of us starting to feel uneasy about this persistent 'digital creep'—that steady march of gadgets and tech into every aspect of our lives. Alas, to the surprise of many, unconsciously, we have even started to assume and feel a little unsettled by how much time we spend staring at screens.

And so, we're beginning to question the assumption that a steady stream of more and newer tech in our lives is an unqualifiedly good thing, and the debate continues, whether it is so or not too many. Yes, it is, or no it is not, comes with a flavour to defined approach to explore success at large with the conscious recognition to the working in particular. In response to this vague sense of tech dis-ease, many of us are looking for a way to think differently about tech and our relationship to it. And there's a sense that maybe this Minimalism thing is the place to start.

References:

https://nickwignall.com/what-is-digital-minimalism/

https://medium.com/swlh/digital-minimalism-how-to-simplify-your-online-life-76b54838a877

https://www.kobo.com/ww/en/ebook/digital-declutter-the-big-checklist-to-obtain-digital-minimalism

https://in.pinterest.com/pin/266345765446875919/

About The Author

Dheeraj Mehrotra, MS, MPhil, PhD (Education Management) honoris causa., a white and a yellow belt in SIX SIGMA, a Certified NLP Business Diploma holder, is an Educational Innovator, Author, with expertise in Six Sigma In Education, Academic Audits, Neuro-Linguistic Programming (NLP), Total Quality Management In Education, an Experiential Educator, a CBSE Resource towards School Assessment (SQAA), CCE, JIT, Five S, and KAIZEN. He has authored over 100 books on topics which include Computer Science, AI, Digital Body Language, NLP, Quality Circles, School Management, Classroom Effectiveness and Safety and security in schools. A former Principal at De Indian Public School, New Delhi, (INDIA), NPS International School, Guwahati, and Education Officer at GEMS, Gurgaon, with an ample teaching experience of over Two Decades, he is a certified Trainer for Quality Circles/ TQM in Education and QCI Standards for School Accreditation/ School Audits and Management. He has also been honoured with the President of India's National Teacher Award in the year 2006 and the Best Science Teacher State Award (By the Ministry of Science and Technology, State of UP), Innovation in Education for his inception of Six Sigma In Education by Education Watch, New Delhi and Education World- Best Teacher Award, BOLT Learner Teacher Award by Air India, 'Innovation in Education Award 2016' by Higher Education Forum (HEF), Gujarat Chapter, among others. He has developed over 150 FREE EDUCATIONAL MOBILE Apps for the Google Play Store exclusively for Teachers, Students, and Parents. This work has been recognised by the LIMCA BOOK OF

RECORDS & INDIA BOOK OF RECORDS as the only Indian to draw that feast. Dr Mehrotra works as a PRINCIPAL at KUNWARS GLOBAL SCHOOL, Lucknow, in India. He has conducted over 1000 workshops globally on "Excellence In Education" integrated with Total Quality Management and Six Sigma, Technology Integration in Education (TIE), Developing towards being ROCKSTAR TEACHERS, including Cyberspace, Cyber Security, Classroom Management, School Leadership & Management, and Innovative teaching within classrooms via Mind Maps, NLP and Experiential Learning in Academics. He is an active TEDx speaker and can be viewed on the youtube TEDx channel. As a premium UDEMY Instructor, he has developed over 450 courses and caters to over 8 Lakh students from 180 countries. He can be visited at www.authordheerajmehrotra.com.

Books By The Same Author

Printed by Libri Plureos GmbH in Hamburg, Germany